FINDING TIME FOR FATHERHOOD

*The important considerations men face
when they become parents*

❖

BRUCE LINTON, PH.D.
Founder of the Fathers' Forum

FATHERS' FORUM PRESS
1521-A Shattuck Ave., Suite 201
Berkeley, CA 94709

Finding Time for Fatherhood: The Important Considerations
Men Face When They Become Parents

Published by
FATHERS' FORUM PRESS
1521-A Shattuck Ave., Suite 201
Berkeley, CA 94709-1516
U.S.A.

Internet Address: www.fathersforum.com

10 9 8 7 6 5 4 3 2 1

Library of Congress Catalog Card Number: 98-96047
ISBN: 0-9649441-0-3

Cover design: Morgan Linton
Cover photograph: Rita LaBarge
Editorial Consultant: Ernest Grafe

Printed by
McNaughton & Gunn
Saline, Michigan
Acid-Free paper

Linton, Bruce, 1950-
Finding Time for Fatherhood: The Important Considerations
Men Face When They Become Parents
p. cm.
1. Fatherhood, 2. Parenting, 3. Men

First Edition: April 1998

Printed in the U.S.A.

CONTENTS

HOW TO USE THIS BOOK

Reading these essays and sharing them with your partner as well as other dads can help you deepen your personal experience of fatherhood. A special feature is the inclusion of questions at the end of each chapter to guide your self-reflection and stimulate discussion.

This book can be used in a number of ways:

❏ Expectant dads and newly "born" fathers — as well as dads with young children — will find this book particularly helpful in developing a personal understanding of the challenges and tensions we encounter as fathers and parents.

❏ Couples will benefit as well, especially allowing mothers to catch a glimpse of the transitions and struggles fathers experience.

❏ Fathers' groups and men's groups will be able to use these essays to stimulate discussions and explore their experiences as fathers and men.

❏ Childbirth and parent educators will find the themes reflected in these essays useful as resource material and as a way to get students thinking about the tensions fathers face in becoming parents.

❏ Obstetricians, pediatricians and family practice physicians will find this book helpful in introducing the dads they encounter to the normal anxieties men experience when they become fathers.

FORWARD

The essays in this book were written over a period of 12 years and appeared in numerous publications in the United States, such as Full-Time-Dads Magazine, for which I was a contributing editor, Children's News in San Francisco, and Nurturing Today, published by David Giveans. Some appeared in newsletters like Neighborhood Moms in Berkeley, California, and The Hispanic-Americans Policeman's Association Newsletter in Florida.

The essays were often written late at night after our kids finally got to bed, or early in the morning when I could steal a few private moments, and I have done minimal editing for this collection. Over the years I have grown as a writer, hopefully, but I felt that the rough edges needed to remain. I hope each essay captures the essence of the issue I was struggling with at that particular stage of fatherhood.

I want to thank Steve Harris, former editor of Full-Time-Dads, for allowing me to contribute to his magazine. I also want to thank the many fathers who have participated in the Fathers' Forum programs; they have been the inspiration for many of the essays. My children and wife have made all these wonderful and difficult experiences of fatherhood possible, and when you read the essays their influences will be obvious.

This is not a "how-to" book. It is a book to stimulate your thinking about what it means to be a father and what value you place in your own life on being a father and a parent.

I hope you might share this book with your partner and friends, and that the essays will encourage further discussions while enhancing your experience of fatherhood.

Bruce Linton, Ph.D.
Founder of the Fathers' Forum
Berkeley, California
February 1998

INTRODUCTION

The evolution of the modern American family, in which both parents are employed, has created the necessity and the opportunity for American fathers to participate more directly in the early years of their children's lives. In the fathers' group that I lead, some men say they never had any close contact with their own fathers, a fact that makes them aware of how important it is to be "present" in their own children's lives. Other fathers say that being with their children feels like a more creative option than potential career advancement.

As new fathers begin to take on more of the day-to-day care of their children, they are entering what traditionally has been perceived as women's territory. Many fathers I have worked with say that after trying to develop a close relationship with their newborns, they find themselves retreating to a more traditional role and fearing that they will become the distant fathers they themselves had. It has become quite clear to me that if men are to develop closer relationships with their children and to be more involved in the workings of their families' daily lives, they have a lot to learn. And men are going to have to help each other out and educate themselves about the deep satisfaction that comes from parenting.

It sometimes seems as if a natural bond between women occurs when they become mothers. Women seem to develop a special deepening of friendship that comes with sharing the experience of motherhood. In contrast, men seem to become isolated from other men as family responsibilities and adjustments are made. Why don't men seek out other fathers for support and advice? Society seems to force men to compete with other men, and they have become intimidated to the point where they are no longer willing to take the risk of making new friendships. As men try to understand their role as fathers, it can seem too overwhelming to reach out to other men. Not having any role models to show them what kind of friendships are available to new fathers leads them to feel that they have to go it alone. Having children — becoming fathers — is such an important event in men's lives, I wonder how they can *not* want to share it with their male friends!

My clinical research has taught me that when men become fathers it is crucial to their adult development to be with other fathers to talk about this important life transition and how it is affecting them. Throughout history, men have had opportunities to share the important events of their lives with other men. It has been an important part of their life experience. Their emotional and psychological well-being has often been anchored in their social relationships with other men. In the last 70 years the industrial and office-oriented work style in America has caused men to become isolated from each other. This becomes particularly problematic when men become fathers. How are fathers to understand all the many emotional and psychological changes they encounter as they become fathers if they have no one to talk with, share with and learn with about all the many changes that parenthood brings?

If men can begin to share their experiences of fatherhood with other dads, they can rekindle the important relationships men need with one another to understand their value as parents. Fatherhood can be the common ground for men to find friendship and emotional connection with each other.

This "re-discovery" of friendships for men through fatherhood is not only of great benefit to men's development as fathers, but will be a positive force for their children, mates, families and ultimately American culture and society.

1

FINDING TIME

I HAVE FOUND IT MOST DIFFICULT to get the time I needed to write this essay! When our children were little, it was obvious why it was impossible to get much "private" time. With small children, the day-to-day tasks are like digging a hole in the sand on the beach; no matter what size the hole, the water will fill it up. The demands of being both physically and emotionally present for infants and young children are pretty much full-time work for both parents.

I have been surprised, even as our children have grown (they are now 12 and 16), that parenting responsibilities are still a major focus of our day-to-day lives. With each year of fatherhood I have had to ask myself, "What kind of father do my children need this year?" I have been lucky in that my personal interest and professional career have been interwoven. I have focused in my career on coaching and counselling parents with young children on how to balance parenting and being a couple with working at jobs and careers. This is also an issue I constantly struggle with myself, and I am not always satisfied with my own results.

As parents, time is our most valuable resource, our most precious commodity. Think about it: We work all our lives so we can retire — in other words, so we can do what we want with our time. The way we define or spend our time defines who we are and what we value.

> *As parents, time is our most valuable resource, our most precious commodity.*

Our society sets values on what we do with our time. I have always been offended by the policy in the United States that if you work and put your kids in childcare, you get a tax credit. But if you stay at home with your children, or work part-time, there is no tax credit. What we say in the U.S. is that we value only your time spent working. How deep the message is in our country that parenting is not a priority.

We do not need to be locked in a battle between time spent working or time spent parenting. Both work time and family time sustain us in very important ways. We gain unique satisfactions from both. And there are practical matters to consider as well: We need money to live, yet our children are only little for such a short time. How will we prioritize our choices?

How we choose to prioritize our time as fathers is very difficult. The undercurrent in our society is still that our identities as men are linked to our work. Although this is changing, careers still provide men with more esteem, status and financial rewards than the time they spend parenting. Also, it is still accepted that the money a man makes is the way he is "supportive" of his family.

Most of the expectant and new fathers I work with are terribly conflicted by wanting to spend time with their young children while having to cope with financial pressures. Even when both parents work, dads as well as moms want more time with their young children. I think we have a much larger social problem then we are aware of in terms of the emotional cost to both parents and young children when it comes to *time* in the early years of parenthood.

From my perspective as a family therapist, it is easy to understand that the changes couples and babies go through in the first year of a child's life depend on having the time to form the necessary attachments that will normally occur. Yet we do little as a society to protect this time for parents or children. Pressures mount quickly for parents to get back to work. I am not saying that every couple should stay home with their new baby. What I am proposing is that, especially in the early years, there is a need for flexibility in regards to time, so that fathers, mothers and baby can feel they have enough time to get to know each other. It takes time to come to a personal understanding of what parenthood and family life mean for each of us as individuals.

> *Each of us . . . needs to find the way to create a work-family balance that can sustain our families emotionally as well as financially.*

In some ways the public problem we have — that we don't provide support for families in our country — must be resolved in a private way. Each of us, as part of a couple and as a parent, needs to find the way to create a work-family balance that can sustain our families emotionally as well as financially. For us as fathers, we need to support each other in parenthood. We dads must give each other the encouragement to take the risks both emotionally and financially to be more integrated in our families.

In choosing our priorities we make sacrifices. If we recognize the gain, the sacrifice is easy. Fathers have been sold a bill of goods when we have been told that our work will give us all the fulfillment we need in life. We are now discovering that we need to feel connected with our children and families to be truly content with life. No father on his deathbed has ever said, "I wish I had spent more time at work."

We are coming to understand as fathers that our relationships with the important people in our lives, especially our children, are of paramount importance to our feeling good about ourselves and to feeling our lives have meaning.

When I asked my children what they think makes a good parent, they gave me the following responses:

Our 12-year-old daughter said that taking kids to school and picking them up (on time), and having time to play with them and help them with their homework, was important. She also commented that young children should spend more time with their parents than a baby sitter.

Our 16-year-old son summed it up by saying it just takes time to spend with your kids. He said people should not be prejudiced against teenage fathers. If they have the time to be with their kids, they can be good fathers too. It all comes down to time.

I know from the dads and new parents I work with, as well as my own wife and me, balancing our many needs and desires and finding the time is often overwhelming. I encourage you not to give up the struggle. Most important, finding the time for your children will not only benefit their development but, particularly for us fathers, will make all the difference in how we feel about what is of real value and meaning in life.

Like the seasons of the year, our lives as parents — as fathers — go through transitions. Look at the time you spend with your children in relationship to the seasons of their lives. Getting your son or daughter off to a good start often takes more time and is very intense. I can't remember how many times I've heard: "They are only little for such a short time." I can't remember any days (or nights) that were longer than when our son and daughter were between birth and two years old. And today I can already feel they have one foot out of our house and into lives of their own. I could not be prouder of each of them, for how wonderful and difficult our life has been, but more than a few times I have wished we could go back in time and my children could be our babies once again.

FOR FURTHER SELF-REFLECTION AND DISCUSSION

1. What do you spend the majority of your time doing?

2. How did your routines change once you had a child? (Or, if you are expecting a baby, how do you *think* your routines will change?)

3. How did your father prioritize his time? What was most important to your father?

2

MEN AND FATHERHOOD: PREGNANCY AND BIRTH

BECOMING A FATHER AND A PARENT can be a transformational process for a man. When a man becomes a father, he comes in contact with a deep paternal masculinity through loving his child, partner and family. When a child enters a man's life, a new depth of feeling and emotion are awakened within him.

In my work with fathers, what I hear new dads talk about most is their interest in being participating and active parents. They want to be able to nurture their child and family by being more than just the breadwinner — as many of their fathers were. They don't want to just put bread on the table for their families, they want to sit down and eat dinner with them too!

A new universe of feelings is awakened in a man through the process of pregnancy and birth. It has been my experience that although women often appreciate this new awakening of feeling in their spouse or partner, they don't really understand what it means to the new or expectant father.

Men's involvement in pregnancy and birth, and their participation in the early years of their children's lives, has changed dramatically over the past 25 years. In 1965, about 5% of fathers attended the birth of a child. In 1989, almost 95% of fathers were present. Men are clearly asking for more participation in the childbirth process. It is also interesting to note that, according to a recent survey on men and work, 75% of the men would accept slower career advancement if they could have a job that would let them arrange their work schedule to have more time with their families.

At the prospect of becoming a father, men are filled with excitement, fear, wonder, worry, love, and confusion. (Just to name a few feelings!) Throughout the pregnancy and birth, the man who is now becoming a father is trying to find ways to express and integrate these and many more feelings.

Pregnancy and Men

Men in western industrialized countries get little preparation in how to make the transition from man to father. Participating in prenatal classes and going to prenatal visits with a partner are ways in which expectant fathers can support their partners/wives and at the same time include themselves in the pregnancy process.

Many men begin during the pregnancy to develop bonds with their children. Expectant fathers in my groups have talked about how they enjoyed laying their hands on their partners' bellies and talking to their babies. This very personal and private communication is very powerful as a prenatal bonding ritual. Helping choose the birth attendants, midwife or doctor and being involved in the choice of where the baby will be born are other ways men begin to become involved. In my work with fathers, through the Fathers' Forum, I see men seeking to understand the journey from man to father, and I see how something very special happens when this search for understanding is shared with other men/fathers. Finding a relationship with other men/fathers during pregnancy is an important way in which we can help initiate each other into fatherhood.

Birth and Fatherhood

Men today want to participate in the birth process. They want to be there with and for their partners. They want to be involved in offering support and love.

Fathers who are able to participate in the birth of their children often report that the sharing of this experience with their partners remains one of the most important moments in their lives. Even if the birth is difficult or a cesarean delivery, men still feel strongly about being together at this special time. A father's importance in participating at the birth is finally getting the acknowledgement it deserves.

Expectant fathers also need to explore what they need at the birth. What kind of support does the expectant dad need to ask for? Many of the new fathers I have worked with talked about how important it was to have a male friend or other father with whom they could talk.

The New Family

"Engrossment" is the term researchers use to describe the father's total absorption and preoccupation with the presence of a newborn. This term could be expanded to describe the early weeks of family life. The first few hours after the delivery are a very important time for the new family to be together. The bonding triangle of mother, father and baby is facilitated by all being together.

The most important aspect of family bonding for new fathers is time. If the new father can have the time to be with his partner and child, the natural process of bonding will take place. There is nothing the father needs to do but spend the time with his new family. As fathers get to know their newborns, they often find a new level of feeling is awakened in them.

This too is an especially important time to be with and talk to other fathers about your experience. It can deepen your own experience as well as validate your growing sense of what being a father is all about. It is important not to be isolated as a new father and to have other resources than your partner to share the many changes new fathers go through. Being in a fathers' group is one way to find affiliation with a group of men.

A father is looking for a psychologically satisfying place within his family. There are many benefits to his involvement in pregnancy, birth and the early years of a child's life. These benefits are not only for his child and wife/partner but for his own understanding of what it is to be man and a father. What I have seen in my work with fathers is that we, as fathers, need to share our experience and support each other. Our dialogue as a community of men helps us understand and appreciate the most important and dynamic life transition: becoming a father.

FOR FURTHER SELF-REFLECTION AND DISCUSSION

1. What training, classes or other preparation did you have for becoming a father?

2. Can you find two other expectant or experienced fathers to meet with, and find out how they feel or felt about the pregnancy of their partners and the birth of their children?

3. After reading this essay, what would be the one question you would like to ask another father about pregnancy or birth?

3

How Having a Baby Changes a Couple's Relationship

W HEN A MAN AND A WOMAN HAVE A BABY, it is a profound transition — the most important change in their adult lives. How becoming parents can affect them as individuals and as a couple is still not well understood in our culture. Of all the Western industrialized countries, the United States offers the least support for family adjustment and development. Politicians would like us to believe that we put a priority on family life, but the reality is just not so. How a man makes the transition to parenthood and how a baby changes a man's relation to his wife are very important areas for us as men to understand.

When a baby is born, the focus of the new mother's attention is on the baby. This is part of the normal developmental process. Mothers become preoccupied with the baby's needs, often to the exclusion of everyone and everything else. This is part of her biological makeup. Most new fathers are unaware of this normal maternal preoccupation and are often surprised and frustrated at how abandoned they may feel. We have no information about what to expect after a baby is born. Men have very little preparation for this intimate part of life. Childbirth preparation classes often help us share with our wives the experience of pregnancy, but we are unaware of what to expect emotionally after the baby arrives. So what's a dad to do?

As a new father feels the emotional withdrawal of his wife's attention, he can take comfort in knowing that her total attentiveness to their baby is normal.

As a new father feels the emotional withdrawal of his wife's attention, he can take comfort in knowing that her total attentiveness to their baby is normal. He can begin to notice whether he has feelings of anger and hurt. Often the time after birth may stimulate unconscious feelings that remind the father of his own childhood. But what about his normal needs for attention and intimacy?

Intellectually, a father can become aware that he is participating in an intimate, common and normal experience of the biological foundation of life. He can take comfort in knowing that as their baby adjusts to being outside rather than inside its mother, this intense connection needs to sustain itself for awhile.

He can also be active in sharing and bonding with his wife and baby by participating in this great mystery of getting to know himself and his wife in their new roles as parents, and becoming acquainted with this new being called their child.

He can begin to get a glimpse of his own vulnerability as the uncertainty of his new role and relationships begin to evolve. Often the new feelings a man uncovers when he becomes a father press him to overwork, perhaps to drink more or to have an affair — all of them ways of trying to escape from the pain of feelings he may be having about the change in relationship with his wife. Even when he is aware of the biological calling for his wife's intense intimacy with the baby, he still feels his own intimate needs neglected.

What I found in my research on new fathers is that throughout history men have had other men — other fathers — with whom to share the transition to parenthood. The joy and loneliness, the fear and confusion were emotions men were able to experience with each other. This was a natural intimacy that men had between them. It is something we have lost in Western industrial countries. Historically, we have always had a community of men friends to turn to at the critical times in our lives. Without this important relationship in a man's life, all his intimacy needs, especially for understanding and comfort, are demanded of his wife and his marriage.

The stereotype persists of men that "they don't share their feelings." What I have found in my work and research is that men don't have opportunities to share their feelings. In my fathers' groups and my all-day workshops we never seem to have enough time to talk, discuss and share all that we want to. The fathers comment on how, unlike their wives — who have many groups available — they have no place to go to specifically talk about the changes they are going through as men and dads.

Not only do we need to be able to establish an intimate relationship with a group of men when we become fathers, but throughout our lives we need the companionship, intimacy and support we can offer each other. Building and maintaining relationships is not easy with the pace and mobility of life today. For us as men to value our male friends, and to work on developing our relationships with each other, takes commitment. Finding ways to create opportunities to be together to talk about the important experiences we are living is of immeasurable value. Having a community of men friends can profoundly effect the quality of our marriages and how our children feel about us as fathers and men. Maybe the loneliness we feel after our babies are born is not just the change in the relationship with our wives, but the sadness we feel at being without any close men to share this most important time in our life.

FOR FURTHER SELF-REFLECTION AND DISCUSSION

1. How has your relationship with your partner changed since you became parents?

2. Do you feel jealous of your partner's relationship with your child?

3. How do you imagine other couples are affected by becoming parents? Do you think, as men, we have any similar experiences as we become fathers?

4

BECOMING A FATHER AND LEARNING ABOUT FRIENDSHIP

I CANNOT REMEMBER, in my childhood or adolescence, ever thinking about being a father. I didn't think about it, in fact, until my late twenties, when my partner of three years, Rita, asked if we should have a baby. She says that was the only time she ever brought up a subject I did not want to talk about. No other subject we have ever discussed (moving, changing jobs, buying a house) made me feel so ambivalent.

I was twenty-nine years old, Rita was twenty-five, and it seemed to be an appropriate time to begin a family. We had both grown up in families of four children. I had recently become licensed as a marriage and family therapist in California. Rita was a registered nurse at our local hospital, and at that time she was working in the nursery. What more could I ask for: A wife who was a nursery nurse!

Although I didn't know it at the time, this was the beginning of my journey to the understanding that by becoming a father I would learn about being a man. I was so confused inside. I found myself faced with what I knew to be one of the most important decisions in my life, and in terrible conflict. How I had been taught to be a man — decisive and in control — went against everything I was feeling inside. How I was taught to be as a man and what I was feeling inside seemed completely opposite. The uncertain and ambivalent feelings that I was taught to suppress and resist in order to be a man were just too strong to be denied. Looking back twelve years, I can now understand that, even before our child had been conceived, something was changing within me.

I had the realization that what I needed was to talk with other fathers.

Typically, I began to explore my decision to become a father by making lists. How would our lives be changed by a child? My lists of positives and negatives grew daily. Finally I became aware that this decision would have to be made with insufficient information. I would have to take a leap of faith. I would need to trust something, as yet unknown, inside myself.

I would need to trust that I could live with fear of the unknown. Fear of not really knowing how our child would change me, my wife, or our marriage. Fear of the emotional and financial responsibilities. Fear that we would not have a healthy baby. Fear of a life that was out of my control. I can now reflect back to this time and appreciate how I was coming to know myself as a man — how control and certainty, traits I had long identified with the "masculine," were merely a facade, a defense against the feelings I was having. I now know those sleepless nights of anxiety about fatherhood were the beginning of learning how to understand my own fear and self-doubts.

Rita and I took the decision to have a baby very seriously. We went away on weekends and questioned and fantasized about what life with a child would be like. What would it be like to be a family? We eventually both came to an important realization. We had hoped to do some travelling as part of our relationship, perhaps extended trips to Europe, China or Nepal. Through our discussions, we came to realize that by having a baby we would not be able to indulge ourselves in travelling the way we had planned. We came to understand that by having a baby we would be doing another type of travelling, an inner journey. We would make discoveries about who we were as parents. At this point, having a child began to feel like an adventure. The hope of pregnancy was transformed into a gift: the miracle of being able to have a baby.

On April 13, 1981, our son Morgan was born. As I held him in my arms in the days that followed his birth, I would often cry. How vulnerable and fragile he seemed. How this little baby would need me! I felt overwhelmed. Was I ready to care for and love this baby? Was I prepared for this most precious of trusts, to nurture a child? How strongly attached to him I felt. How lost I felt about what I was to do as a father.

I was up with him one night when he was about a week old — it was probably about 2:00 A.M. — and I had turned the radio on. As the announcer read the news, I recall being profoundly concerned about the state of affairs in the world. The world needed to be a safe, welcoming place for my son. War, poverty, crime — these problems needed to be solved . . . immediately!

My son, one week old, was already bringing me into contact with the world in a new way. New feelings of concern and compassion were being born within me. Since his birth eleven years ago, my interest in the environment, schools, the economy and public safety has grown vitally alive within me. It was as if my personal sense of isolation was coming to an end and a new feeling for community began to develop.

I was proud and excited to become a dad, but I also felt overwhelmed and bewildered about my life. My wife and I talked about our experiences together, but something was missing for me. I began to realize that she had many women friends with whom she could talk about what it was like to be a mother. I discovered that I had no men friends with whom I could talk and share my feelings about being a father.

I had the realization that what I needed was to talk with other fathers. I needed to hear from other dads how they were coping with all the changes in their lives and relationships.

This has been one of the most important insight for me as a father: *I need to be with other fathers.* This insight led me to help form a group for new fathers. The impact of this small group of men took me out of my isolation and also helped me have a forum for the feelings I was either trying or longing to express to my wife. Here in this group of men I had a home for all my confusion and bewilderment about myself as a new father. Here was a place for me to come and understand myself as a father — and as a man.

FOR FURTHER SELF-REFLECTION AND DISCUSSION

1. Who are your two closest male friends?

2. What efforts do you make to keep in contact with your friends?

3. As a father and a parent, what is important for you to share with another friend/father?

5

FATHERS AND MARRIAGE

THE MOST IMPORTANT THINGS IN LIFE ARE NOT THINGS! Our relationships are! The relationship that has had the most impact on our own lives is the one we had with our parents. By the same token, our relationship with our partners — our marriages — will influence our children in many profound ways.

Providing good schools, living in a decent neighborhood, participating in community and sports activities, having a computer, offering music lessons — these are some of the ways we help to nurture our kids as they grow and develop. Every father wants his child to grow up to be an honest and caring person. But how does that happen?

If we reflect on our own parent's marriage, what was it like? Did they treat each other with dignity and respect? Were they considerate and understanding with each other? How did they handle the inevitable anger and frustration that comes not just with parenting, but with life! Did they seem to enjoy being married? Why did they have children?

The relationship between husband and wife is the center of a child's developing morality. How he treats himself and others grows out of the observations he makes of the way his parents treat each other.

Many men who become fathers today take pride in their involvement, right from birth, in the nurturing and caring of their infants.

The relationship between husband and wife is the center of a child's developing morality.

This is a very positive change in our culture. Fathers' involvement in active parenting is creating a new model for family life.

I am always struck by meeting fathers who are so positively engaged with and excited about their children, but appear so uninterested in or disengaged from their relationships with their wives. I often comment to couples I see in my psychotherapy practice that they act like single parents who are living together. Everything in their relationship seems to focus on their child.

In many cases, as time goes on, the parents begin to work out many of their interpersonal difficulties through their children. Young children may begin to wonder why their parents seem to have so much love for them and not seem to care much about each other. What does an experience like that teach a child about interpersonal relationships?

There is a great renaissance today for men, and today's father is the cornerstone. A new developing sense of masculinity and gender identity is unfolding around the development of the nurturing father. It is important, rewarding and valuable to participate in the caregiving to our children. But if we don't also nurture our marriage, what have we really conveyed to our children about being a loving and caring person? One of the greatest gifts a father can give to his children is to love his wife. This is a lovely statement, but in reality a difficult and often life-long adventure in understanding another person. Good luck!

FOR FURTHER SELF-REFLECTION AND DISCUSSION

1. What is most difficult for *you* about loving another person?

2. What are the trade-offs in being married? (What do you find liberating about being married, or in a committed relationship, and what is restricting?)

3. What can *you* do in your relationship that would have a positive effect without your mate changing her behavior or personality?

6

The Structure of Fatherhood: Looking Beyond Our Personal Fathers

Wहेन men become fathers, they are confronted with a profound challenge to understand what being a "father" means to them. Most men are perplexed by this. In both my personal and professional lives, I have searched to understand why becoming a father is such an uncertain experience for today's men.

In the fathers' groups I have led, most men look to their own fathers as examples of how to be parents. Reflecting on their own fathers' behavior often leaves them feeling sad, lonely, frustrated, angry and ambivalent. In our group, together, we struggle to understand and make peace with our own fathers. Many of the men in my groups feel very limited by having a father who was either physically or emotionally absent from their lives. We try to understand how we can be more available and more emotionally connected with our families. Some of the men who had abusive fathers become fearful and wonder if they might hurt their own children. If we must rely on our own personal fathers as teachers or mentors on parenting, we may feel limited. To understand himself as a man, each of us must come to an understanding of his own father and his father's influence on his life, both positive and negative.

> *Many of the men in my groups feel very limited by having a father who was either physically or emotionally absent from their lives.*

However, I question the limitation of understanding one's own father as a path to becoming a more nurturing parent. We have to look beyond our fathers. Where must we look to gain a broader perspective about what it means to be a father?

The idea of an original model after which similar things are patterned — a kind of prototype — is what the depth-psychologist Carl Jung called an archetype. I thought there would have to be a prototype for what it means to be a father, but I was surprised by what I discovered.

There is an archetype for motherhood. The "Madonna and Child" image appears in some form throughout the world. The biological basis of pregnancy and giving birth sets up a relationship between mother and child that is, to varying degrees, stable in all parts of the world. This is not the case for fatherhood. Images of fathers and their relationships with their children and families are not stable, and vary widely from culture to culture. If this is true, what does it tell us about the meaning of fatherhood?

To begin with, it seems to indicate that fatherhood is

socially constructed. Depending upon the culture, the historical time and the needs of the society, fathers may play a variety of roles. It is both a frightening and liberating thought that fathers have no prototypic model for how to be parents. This means that men can stop looking towards (and perhaps blaming) their own fathers for instruction (or lack thereof) on how to be fathers. They can begin to explore within themselves and in the world at large for the kinds of behavior and family life they would like to provide for their own children. They must turn to each other, father to father, and learn together how to develop positive nurturing relationships with their children.

Each father, in his own way, must search out and discover what kind of father he wants to be for his children.

Understanding what it means to be a father is a very personal journey for each and every one of us. Each father, in his own way, must search out and discover what kind of father he wants to be for his children. It is a difficult journey and many men shy away from questioning what it means to be a father. For those who are willing to take the journey, it is surely a path filled with heartfelt expectations. Hopefully it is a path shared with fellow fathers where, at this time in history, we can help each other along the way. Perhaps never before have we as fathers had such an opportunity to consciously participate in the lives of our children.

It's a great time to be a father. Seize the moment!

FOR FURTHER SELF-REFLECTION AND DISCUSSION

1. What was most difficult for your father in his life?

2. How did your father fail you in your life, and how was he there for you?

3. If you were to write a letter to your father about how you feel about him as your dad, what would it say?

$$\boxed{7}$$

NURTURING FATHERS

W<small>E ALL WANT TO BE NURTURING PARENTS</small>. Most fathers today want to reassure their children that they are loved. Many men grew up with fathers who were not very demonstrative, and often felt as if they had to earn their father's love. It is important for men to show their children they love them, not only for their children's sake but for their own as well. Fathers demonstrate their love for their children by being available to them, by being actively involved in their care and upbringing, and by supporting their personal interests. This type of engagement with their children often reflects how men wish their own fathers had been involved with them. Certainly participating in children's lives does convey love, but beyond that fathers must be able to prepare their children for the complexities of the world. In this sense, "love is not enough."

In 1950, the child psychologist Bruno Bettelheim wrote a book called *Love is Not Enough*, in which he says: "Fortunately, most parents love their children and conscientiously strive to be good parents. But more and more of them become weary of the struggle to arrange life sensibly for their children, while modern pressures create more and more insensible experiences which are added to the life of the child." This passage, written in 1950, has only become truer with the passing of time. Fatherhood involves more than just time and love. To be able to raise healthy children, fathers must be able to help them navigate through the stresses and "insensible" experiences of life. This is particularly true when the children are young.

> *My definition of nurturing fathers centers around the fathers' ability to help anticipate their children's emotional needs.*

My definition of nurturing fathers centers around the fathers' ability to help anticipate their children's emotional needs. This means that they must be able to translate with some accuracy their children's emotional environment. Children's television shows like *Sesame Street* and *Mr. Rogers Neighborhood* do a good job of understanding children's emotions. Both of these shows have talked about the fears children have when they start school, what it feels like when their parents fight, and how to handle disappointment. The programs offer comforting, reassuring examples of how a child can cope with these situations, and this can truly reduce a child's anxiety.

Adults often feel stressed and emotionally fatigued, leaving them little energy to sympathize with their children's stress. Parents need to examine their own ability to balance and juggle the many tasks of life so that they can be genuinely available to their children. No one needs to tell fathers how to love their children. The devotion and affection fathers feel for their children is a profound kind of love, but it is not enough. Today' s fathers need to be able to anticipate the stresses and pressures that impinge on their children's lives. If they can do that, they may not be able to remove these stresses but they may be able to soften them a bit. As children grow, they will develop the strength and resiliency they need to master these situations and learn from their fathers that life's difficulties are not a burden but an adventure!

FOR FURTHER SELF-REFLECTION AND DISCUSSION

1. What do you do that lets your children know you love them?

2. Even if you have a newborn, what do you know about your child's unique emotional needs?

3. When you are tired or fatigued, how do you respond to your child needs?

8

FATHER'S DAY

WHEN WE ACKNOWLEDGE FATHER'S DAY, what are we celebrating? Is it a personal tribute to our fathers? Is it the commemoration of male parentage? Of all the major holidays, Father's Day is the least observed and celebrated. Perhaps because men's relationships with their own fathers are often difficult, they feel reluctant to honor a day in their dads' behalf. In my work with fathers, I find that the number of men who want to honor their fathers on this day is equal to the number of men who want to mourn their relationships with their fathers. It seems that Father's Day is bittersweet national holiday, evoking both the admiration and disdain that men (and women) feel about their fathers.

As men become fathers, celebrating this day can become very intense emotionally. I feel that men undervalue how profoundly they may be affected by this institutionalized ritual of acknowledging fatherhood. There is much denial in our society and in our personal lives about fatherhood. All men hope for fathers who can support them in both their physical and emotional needs. Young children want to trust the adults who are responsible for them. Parents are often not prepared or are not aware of how to "be there" for their kids.

Being there for your children means giving them your time and attention. Focusing on their needs and feelings, and helping children cope with their disappointments and excitements, is the core of parenting. This is true for fathers and mothers both!

We can dedicate ourselves on this Father's Day to transforming the paternal bond between ourselves and our families into a nurturing, cooperative and vitally alive connection.

What happens to children when their fathers either are not or cannot be there for them? Research indicates that children of absent fathers do less well socially and academically. They may also have more difficulties in interpersonal relationships. It is not just having a male parent in the house that is important. It is the ability of the father to be nurturing, warm and caring for his child. That is what fathering is all about.

Many men can look back on their lives and find adults who were not their biological dads but who supported them, coached them, and were "mentor fathers." It is natural for children to seek out adults who can take pride in their achievements and convey to them that they are special and unique.

How men interact with their children and their mates, and how they feel about themselves as men, leaves a lasting impression on their children. Children's attitudes reflect the possibilities their parents see for themselves. Children learn the limitations of life and their own potential by watching how their parents deal with daily life — from how they greet the day to how they cope with disappointment and loss.

As we reflect on Father's Day this year, let us appreciate that, even if we were very wounded by our own fathers, we can be more substantial, more present in our children's lives than we felt our fathers were in ours. We can honor all the fathering influences who have contributed to our lives. We can dedicate ourselves on this Father's Day to transforming the paternal bond between ourselves and our families into a nurturing, cooperative and vitally alive connection. Let us thank our children and let them know how proud we are of them and how lucky we feel to be their fathers on this Father's Day.

FOR FURTHER SELF-REFLECTION AND DISCUSSION

1. What did you do for Father's Day last year?

2. How was Father's Day celebrated when you were a child?

3. How would you like your Father's Day to be acknowledged?

4. Aside from your biological father, who were or are the other "fathers" in your life?

9

A New Interpretation of an Old Myth: Oedipus Rex Reconsidered

Sigmund Freud was a physician whose interest in neurology led to the development of modern psychology. He used the Oedipus Rex story from Greek mythology to express how strongly young boys may be attached to their mothers' love. He felt that this story explained what he considered to be an unconscious process in which a young boy rejects his father so that he can have his mother's love all to himself. The Oedipal complex and the Oedipal phase of development have become commonplace in the terminology of childhood psychology. Working through the Oedipal phase, young boys separate from their mothers and begin to develop their sense of themselves as men. Unfortunately, if one accepts the traditional interpretation of Freud, it means that boys must reject their mothers (and the femininity which their mothers represent) in order to develop their own identity and masculinity.

This not only devalues mothers and women but cuts off boys' connections to the feminine principal, which limits their development of a more whole and well-rounded psychological/emotional life.

Let's reconsider the Oedipal myth. The story *Oedipus Rex* is about King Laius and Queen Jocasta of Thebes. Laius learns of a prophecy from the Oracle of Delphi that he and his wife will have a son who will kill his father and marry his mother. When their son is born, Laius has the newborn child left on a hillside to die so that the prophecy cannot be fulfilled.

New fathers often report feelings of jealousy because of all the attention the baby is getting and the neglect they feel as a result.

The infant boy, Oedipus,* is found by a shepherd and raised by King Polybus of Corinth. Oedipus hears the prophecy as a man and leaves Delphi and Corinth, fearing that he will kill Polybus, who he believes to be his real father. On his journey Oedipus encounters an arrogant, rich nobleman who orders him off the road. Oedipus kills the man, who turns out to be Laius, in a duel. Oedipus ends up outside the city of Thebes, which is terrorized by a Sphinx and can only be saved by someone who can answer the Sphinx's riddle. Oedipus answers the riddle, the Sphinx kills herself and Oedipus is honored by the whole city. Queen Jocasta has lost her husband and Oedipus is deemed a good match for her, so they marry, fulfilling the prophecy. When Oedipus becomes aware that the prophecy has come true, he blames himself for all that has happened and blinds himself.

---

* The name Oedipus means "wounded foot," a refrence to the story that Laius deliberately injured his infant son's foot so he could not escape from the hillside.

In my interpretation, this myth says more about fathers than it does about boys. It is the father who is jealous and fearful that his son will marry his wife and become king. The father is worried that his son will replace him, and this is what motivates him to attempt to kill his own child. It seems more like a father-son complex to me than a mother-son problem. Why doesn't the father protest the prophecy? Why does Freud choose to ignore the father's conscious and cruel behavior toward his son?

In working as a psychotherapist with couples who have young children, I find that the Oedipal theme of the father's jealousy is common. Many men were the primary focus of their mate's attention prior to the birth of their child. New fathers often report feelings of jealousy because of all the attention the baby is getting and the neglect they feel as a result. New fathers often have a conscious wish to go back to the relationship they had before the baby was born. Helping couples develop into a family and adjust to being parents requires having fathers come to terms with these feelings of jealousy, abandonment and lack of attention from their mates.

I think it is time to re-examine the Oedipal myth in terms of what it is saying about a father's unconscious feelings regarding the early stages of parenthood. The fear of a son or daughter becoming the primary recipient of his mate's attention and affection, and the possibility that the child will replace him as the "king" within the family, are very difficult concepts for a new father.

In Freud's interpretation, fathers can displace their own emotional difficulties onto their children and then punish them for the normal loving relationship that exists between mothers and children. Projecting onto innocent children the feeling of wanting to murder their father for desiring their mother's love appears to me to reflect more on a father's fears and jealousies than anything else.

As fathers today, we need to recognize the mythology that has guided our development. As we create a new definition of fatherhood, we must examine the fears and educate ourselves about aggressive feelings that becoming parents stirs within us. We must come to terms with our own emotional projections and breathe new meaning into a mythology that honors our children and mates. It may not be an easy task to reflect on our own emotional vulnerabilities, but it is one we can help each other with as we grow and develop in our relationships and lives.

FOR FURTHER SELF-REFLECTION AND DISCUSSION

1. Are you jealous of the relationship between your partner and your baby? If so, how does the jealousy manifest itself?

2. How do you handle the frustration when your child's needs must come before your needs?

3. When you were growing up, how did your mother and father reconcile their needs as individuals and as a couple with your needs as a child?

10

CHRISTMAS

THE HOLIDAY SEASON BRINGS UP A VARIETY OF FEELINGS FOR FAMI-LIES, from joy to dread. The pressures of our consumer society can make this a tense time of year. Crowded stores and traffic jams all add to the flurry of activity that often pushes us to the limits of our patience. We find ourselves asking the question, Is it really worth it? Could we do without this "holiday madness?" Couldn't we just skip the whole thing?

It is up to us as parents (or us as dads) to rescue Christmas from its commercialism and restore it as one of the special days in our children's lives. We can help create a special time of year to celebrate children, which I believe was the original intent of this holiday.

For most children, Christmas is not a religious holiday. Children don't associate a jolly fat man in a red suit with any religious symbolism. As my daughter once said, it is quite exciting to have a tree in the house. When our children were young, the surprise on their faces when they found their presents under the tree made it clear how special the experience was for them.

Christmas is a celebration of children. As I researched the history of St. Nick, I was led to his pre-Judeo-Christian past. It appears Santa Claus has his origins in a pre-Christian deity who was the protector of children, a nature spirit similar to the "green man" whose job it was to look out for the welfare of children. Both Hanukkah and Christmas may have been adjusted to coincide with this earlier folk tradition, which was the focus of the winter season.

> *It is up to us as parents . . . to rescue Christmas from its commercialism and restore it as one of the special days in our children's lives.*

Children, especially young ones, need to have special days that are just for them. Except for school graduations and religious ceremonies that mark memorable moments in their lives, children have few special days of their own. Only birthdays and Christmas remain as days truly reserved for kids. If these days are diminished in importance, children lose some of life's joy and the good feelings that go with it.

Santa Claus reaches out to children in a unique way. Presents and giving can certainly express love and good will at this time of year. Most children know Santa doesn't bring gifts to parents. Somehow, Santa Claus is just for them. For children who believe in the Santa Claus story, Christmas can be a magical time that brings much personal happiness.

Children who can experience the ancient myth of Santa Claus have their lives immensely enriched. The thought of a good, happy, colorfully dressed person who brings presents just for them creates a sense and magic in their lives. While difficulties and uncertainties in life are many, Christmas and the magic of Santa Claus help reassure children and give them a sense of hope. If our rational thinking forces us to deprive our children of the symbolic meaning that Santa represents, we lose the beneficial effects that can extend over the lifetime of the child.

Children have a need for magical thinking. From about four to ten years old, magical thinking actually helps kids cope with the world. The hardships, difficulties, even terrors that are part of our lives — which we cope with as adults — can be dealt with by young children through magical beliefs. Magical thinking declines as children grow and their rational consciousness is equipped to deal with the uncertainties and vicissitudes of life.

If our rational thinking forces us to deprive our children of the symbolic meaning that Santa represents, we lose the beneficial effects that can extend over the lifetime of the child.

Together, my wife and I have tried to craft a unique Christmas for our children. We have a great time choosing a tree and decorating it. Our tree is covered with ornaments the kids have made over the years. Our children feel the joy of getting gifts that are given in celebration of them, with no one but Santa to thank.

As our children have gotten older, we have begun to explore the meaning of "peace" at this time of year. This is a time when we can all wish for a world that is more nurturing and peaceful. Our children can begin to express the feelings of gratitude that reflect their own experience of Christmas and what it means to them.

The winter solstice, the seasonal change, begins to mark a time of turning inward. With less daylight, the cold, the change in the landscape around us, we all feel some of the seasonal transition. Connecting with these changes is part of the experience of Christmas for us, too. My wife and I take pleasure in creating a meaningful time for us to enjoy being a family together.

FOR FURTHER SELF-REFLECTION AND DISCUSSION

1. What do you find most difficult about the holiday season?

2. How did your family celebrate Christmas when you were a child?

3. How would you like to celebrate Christmas, and how can you talk about it with your partner?

11

EDUCATING OUR CHILDREN

As SEPTEMBER APPROACHES AND SUMMER DRAWS TO AN END, parents begin to prepare their children (and themselves) for school. I can still remember my son's first day at kindergarten, nine years ago. Taking him to school, my wife and I were nervous as we reassured him that school would be fun. We often referred to Sesame Street and how Big Bird was afraid on the first day of school, too. We were proud as well as anxious about this important beginning and transition. All the parents escorted their children to the class, which would be in session from eight to twelve o'clock. The room was brightly decorated with craft projects, a large alphabet around the tops of all four walls, art easels and boxes of puppets and dress-up clothes. It really felt upbeat and fun! Then the parents went for coffee and tea with the principal in an assigned room. The principal reassured us that in his fifteen years of being principal of this school, every single parent had made it through the first day just fine!

Participating in school activities with my children, escorting field trips, being a room parent, being a helper in the class and assisting with school fairs and fund-raising have all been rich experiences for me as a father. They have helped me to feel as though I were a part of a community and have introduced me to many new friends I would not have met otherwise.

> *I have found that it is simple to say that fathers should be more involved in their children's education, but many dads have difficulty arranging this.*

Aside from my eighth-grade, high school and college graduations, I never saw my father or any other father that I can remember at school activities. I think my involvement with my own children has helped me to heal my own loneliness and longing for my father to show an interest in my activities. I also believe that my children have benefitted enormously from my participation. School and all the activities associated with it take up an enormous amount of every child's life. The interest you show in what is a major part of their lives — a part that can also cause them worry and fear — comforts them by showing them that you care.

Participating in my children's schooling has let them know that I value their education, that school is important and that I make it a priority in my life. It has been reassuring for them to have a father who is familiar with the children in their class, and I believe that it has allowed them to feel more comfortable in school. I feel that my involvement in the early years of my children's education helped them feel more confident in school. In fact, research in the field of child development shows that there is a positive correlation between fathers' involvement in their children's education and their children's academic and social development. I have been very fortunate to have had the experience of being able to play an active role in my children's education. Many other fathers I know would like to be more involved but are prevented from doing so. For various reasons, fathers cannot always do all the things they would like to do for their children. Many questions arise: Where can sacrifices be made, what trade-offs can be made, and how much money can be given up for the time that would be gained? If parents work less and participate more in their children's early years, how does that affect their ability to save for their children's college years or provide for their own needs later in life?

I have found that it is simple to say that fathers should be more involved in their children's education, but many dads have difficulty arranging this. I am sure that all of the men who attend my programs for fathers would like to be able to spend more time with their children, especially in terms of involvement with their children's education. It appears to me that parents' economic class levels determine how much or how little they can be involved directly with their children. Self-employed professionals seem to have more flexibility than blue collar workers or corporate employees, for example, while parents in management or ownership positions seem to be able to cre-

> *In all daily interactions there are opportunities for children to learn many of the important lessons of life.*

ate more flexible hours. Society in general tends to discount fathers' interest in their children and to pay little attention to the difficulties they may have in balancing their work lives and their home lives.

As parents get ready to send their children off to various schools, they should look for ways to get involved with their children's education. Perhaps the limited definition of education in this society should be expanded. In all daily interactions there are opportunities for children to learn many of the important lessons of life. I believe in this principle on a very personal level. Fairness and patience are themes that we stress at our house. Honesty and respect are not just values that my wife and I believe in, but values we practice through actions and discussion with our family and friends.

> *Parents have many unique experiences and interests, all of which can enrich their children's lives.*

Parents today have many opportunities to participate in their children's education. Supporting children in their school work and formal education is certainly an important area, but there are also many opportunities in day-to-day life for parents to share their knowledge and to educate their children. Reading to your child at night, looking at the newspaper together and going to movies and plays are all ways of bringing about stimulating discussions between you and your child. Parents have many unique experiences and interests, all of which can enrich their children's lives.

No matter how busy their schedules are, parents need to rearrange them to allow some time *each* day to be with their children and to be their children's guides and mentors. Time can pass very quickly. Tomorrow goes by too soon, and tod-dlers are teens in the blink of an eye. *Today* is when parents have to start, and now is the best time of all. One of the most important things that parents can teach their children is how valuable they are, by making time for them each day. And this lesson is something they in turn will pass on to their children.

FOR FURTHER SELF-REFLECTION AND DISCUSSION

1. How do you help prepare your child for school emotionally?

2. What will you do so learning takes place at home and school?

3. How can you make learning fun, an enjoyable experience for your children no matter what their age?

12

FATHERHOOD AND
THE MEN'S MOVEMENT

W<small>HAT IS GOING ON IN THE MEN'S MOVEMENT?</small> Do we really
need a movement? Since most of the institutions in our society are designed and controlled by men, what do we really
want to change?

War, incest, poverty, racism and the relationship between
men and women are not separate and independent issues but
interconnected and part of our societal value system.

Any men's movement that does exist owes a great debt to
the women's movement and the development of feminist phi-
losophy/ psychology in the United States. For more than twen-
ty years women have been championing the causes of equality
and equity both in the work world and in family life. They
have led the struggle to improve education and childcare.

Today's media-driven men's movement has ignored fatherhood. This has been my personal experience as I have partici-

pated in groups and workshops over the past twenty-five years, and it was one of the reasons for starting the Father's Forum in 1986. (The Father's Forum offers men's groups for fathers as well as workshops for new and expectant dads.) In groups with Robert Bly and Michael Mead, and in my own men's groups and activities here in Northern California, I found a wonderful community of men. I discovered that the competitiveness and isolation I was taught to value was keeping me from being part of a community. The losses I carried within and never expressed were slowly eating me up from the inside. I began to understand how the unconscious devaluing of women had cut me off from a more nurturing part of myself. Through myth and stories, but mostly in the care of men — some older, some younger — I found a place to tell my stories. I became aware of how little opportunity I had had to talk about life, the struggles of my own experiences, with other men. This is the greatest gift of the men's movement — to have the opportunity to safely talk with other men about the inner experiences of day-to-day living. This is the most healing and politically radical change the men's movement has created.

Today's media-driven men's movement has ignored fatherhood.

It was not until I had children myself that I began to realize that the issues of being a father and having a family were not being addressed by my "men's work." Talking about what it means to be a man is important, but if it does not connect us to the greater issues of our lives, then the men's movement is a failure. If the men's movement causes a greater schism than already exists between men and women, then it has failed doubly.

I think the most vital aspect of today's men's movement — and the least publicized and understood — is fatherhood. A fundamental shift is taking place in our society. We are aspiring to transform from a dominator to a partnership culture. Here we find the sharing of work and home life, making money and raising children becoming a cooperative endeavor by men and women.

What today's fathers are doing all over the country is a grass roots political movement. When men become fathers, an opportunity for a profound and fundamental emotional shift in consciousness can occur. The vulnerability of their children can touch their own fears and vulnerabilities, and an emotional awakening can occur. This awakening is not just to the world of feelings. It is a connection to the world of greater political realities that they must now struggle with. It is the experience of "generativity" that carries the father from his own concerns about his identity as a man to the greater concerns for his family and community.

When men become fathers, an opportunity for a profound and fundamental emotional shift in consciousness can occur.

For years the men's movement has attempted to help men go from the narcissism of what it means to be a man to a more dynamic involvement in our society. Today's fathers are fulfilling this aspiration. Our sense of manhood, what kind of person we want to be — beyond gender definition — is what today's dads struggle with. I see it over and over again in my father's groups. Men are reintegrating the nurturing and generative aspects of their emotional lives, and are coming to terms with a new definition of what it means to be a man, a definition which includes how to contribute to a society worthy of bringing children into.

Understanding what it takes to be a parent, the sleepless nights and endless patience, feeling the fears and vulnerabilities of having young children, worrying about education and childcare, figuring out how to provide guidance, setting limits without injuring your child's spirit, living equitably with your partner, being a parent and a husband, crafting a loving marriage and a family with values, morals and ethics — these are the challenges for today's dads. Sharing these struggles with other men/fathers helps create a community of men who are not only raising their consciousness about being men but about the society we live in.

It is my hope that as the respective men's and women's movements continue to develop, we will see that our similarities outweigh our differences. We can live together as allies and raise children who will reflect all the best of what it means to be not just men or women but truly caring human beings.

FOR FURTHER SELF-REFLECTION AND DISCUSSION

1. Are men and women being socialized differently? How so?

2. What "feminine" qualities do you feel would help you as a man?

3. Are there subtle ways you devalue women, or do you deal with the men and women in your life equally?

13

DADS AND EDUCATION

When I originally wrote this essay (1995) and sent it to Steve, editor of Full-Time-Dads, I found out that I had not written on the subject he had requested. Fortunately, I had a few days to work on another essay. Unfortunately, school was starting for our kids. Our son Morgan was starting Berkeley High School and our daughter Julia was starting fourth grade at Sierra School. The beginning of school is both an exciting and anxious time. Luckily, the essay I was suppose to write was on how we as dads can participate in our children's education.

Personally, I was hoping to get this article finished last night, but my daughter and I had to go over her math and my son needed me to help him get ready for a quiz on the Middle East. I think one of the ways I support my kids in their educational endeavors is to be able to put aside my work to help them with theirs. Showing interest as fathers in our children's school work means so much for so many reasons.

In our culture (not that I agree with this, and I am glad it is changing), we tend to value more or give greater status to what men do. When we put aside all the "important" things that dads have to do and show our interest and desire to help our kids with school work, we transfer this cultural esteem to their activity. This can have both posi-

I think dads serve a very important and primary function of valuing education and conveying this to their children.

tive and negative consequences.

Positively, our interest lets us show we feel what they are doing is important. But if our children feel criticized or pressured by our interest, they can feel shamed — as if they weren't good enough for their fathers. Oftentimes, in working with fathers in my psychotherapy practice, I find that dads have their hearts in the right place, but they may come across to their children as too rigid in their desire to help. The dad's need to see his child be successful sometimes overshadows the needs of his child.

I consulted with our fourteen-year-old son on this subject, and he gave me some interesting insights. Morgan thought that being supportive did not always mean helping out with the specifics of the homework. He believed that listening to what he was doing and how he was doing it, without too much input, was most valuable. Mistakes would be there, but the overall experience of my interest and excitement about his work was better than helping with a lot of corrections. Great advice from a fourteen-year-old, certainly for us dads of adolescents!

I think dads serve a very important and primary function of valuing education and conveying this to their children, especially in the home. Other attitudes that dads express, such as reassurance and confidence in their children's abilities in general, will add to their children's preparation for dealing with the many social obstacles that occur at school. Learning often begins with being able to feel comfortable enough about yourself to take in what goes on in class. A father's confidence in his child goes a long way in promoting a positive academic experience.

If possible, it's great to be involved at your child's school. Young kids, especially, love to see their dads at school. Last year I was a room parent for Julia's third-grade class and loved being an integral part of her day-to-day school life. Several other dads I know come regularly to help out in class. Field trips, school festivals and back-to-school nights are also opportunities to be part of your child's education in an important community, rather than academic, way.

Many of the men I know would love to be more involved in their kids' school days, but lack of job flexibility makes it very difficult, and in some cases impossible.

It is important to mention that many of the men I know would love to be more involved in their kids' school days, but lack of job flexibility makes it very difficult, and in some cases impossible, to make the commitments they desire. Being creative and strategic in choosing the activities you can be involved in is important. Don't give up if you have a restrictive or rigid employment.

Finally, express your interest in education by continuing to educate yourself. Lectures, classes, reading books and talking about your own new learning are powerful incentives for your children. Look for small opportunities to share educational experience together. (Museums, art galleries and community centers are often good sources.)

But most important, make time to listen to what school is like for your kids. Hear both their academic and social learnings. Try and understand what it is like for them to "be" in school. The fears and anxieties that come up in school are often as difficult to understand and master as math and spelling.

FOR FURTHER SELF-REFLECTION AND DISCUSSION

1. When you were growing up, what was your parents' attitude toward education?

2. What unique talents or skills do you see in your child?

3. How can you participate in your child's education?

14

FOOD FOR THOUGHT

EDUCATING OURSELVES ABOUT PARENTING is a critical part of our being "good enough" fathers. Understanding the importance of food and the need for independence among small children is basic to helping them develop good eating habits and self esteem.

Many of the difficulties I see with dads of teenagers and families with adolescents are issues that began in early childhood as struggles around food. As a family therapist, one of the areas I want to discuss when a family comes in for treatment is its food and eating routines.

For young children, how often and how much they eat can vary greatly. Young children's appetites are not organized around the adults' defined eating times. As adults we have learned — as children do over time — to be organized around eating three times a day. Our external and internal rhythms are now structured around these times. Young children are much more internally focused. A three-year-old can not want anything to eat at noon and by twelve-thirty be ravishingly hungry. A young child focusing on play may find lunch time (and food) an unwelcome intrusion.

Young children's need for independence is often met with great ambivalence. Eating is a way they may experiment with

Young children's appetites are not organized around the adults' defined eating times.

this confusion. Acting out around food is one way a young child tries to understand and master his need for independence and autonomy. What he puts in his mouth and how much he eats and when he eats are among the few ways he can exercise independent control in his life. Children can eat huge meals one day and not be hungry at all the next. They can love a special food one week and refuse to eat it a week later. Sometimes a child may want to be totally catered to, while at other times the same child may want to be left alone.

While all dads would like their children to enjoy eating, each parent brings his or her own hang-ups to this area. Usually there are unresolved issues from our own childhood that we react to in our children. If you remember your own past experiences around eating, you need not continue them with your children. Forcing a child to eat is a certain road to eating problems. In order for a child to enjoy eating, he or she must be in control.

Toddlers will often use food to test limits. They will always want the food you don't have. You can let your child know that "This is what we have for dinner tonight. We will

have [whatever the child is asking for] tomorrow night."
Parents need to learn to relax around meal times. Children's
nutritional needs are fairly simple, and you are probably
doing just fine if your child falls within the normal ranges
for weight and height and if the available food is generally
nutritious.

If you haven't made food a struggle for both you and your
children, by the time they are four or five they will find it
exciting to try new foods and experiment with new tastes.
Establishing independence about eating is one way in which
we help our child learn their own limits and foster their ability to make their own choices, an
essential ingredient in positive
self-esteem. Pickiness, refusal of
certain foods, wide variation in
tastes from one week to the next,
are all part of the normal phases
kids go through. Tolerance is
what we need to learn — and
show — as parents.

Of course, if your child
refuses to eat over a prolonged
period or is very thin or over-
weight, it would be appropriate
to seek your doctor's advice.

Respecting our children's
need for control, and being
aware of our own eating history, we can proceed into the
future with our families in a relaxed and positive manner at
meal times.

I hope this has been some food for thought.

> *If you haven't
> made food a
> struggle for both
> you and your
> children, by the
> time they are four
> or five they will
> find it exciting to
> try new foods and
> experiment with
> new tastes.*

FOR FURTHER SELF-REFLECTION AND DISCUSSION

1. What are the "feeling tones" at your meals? Tense or relaxed?

2. How flexible or rigid are you about your child's eating?

3. When you were growing up, what were the rules about food and eating? What was the mood around the dinner table with your parents?

15

THE RITES OF SPRING: HARDBALL, SOFTBALL AND GENDER.

FOR THE LAST SIX YEARS I have been involved in coaching boys' Little League and girls' softball. Everything starts in January, when I fill out the application and make sure it gets mailed on time. Then I look at the team schedule for the season and figure out how I will adjust *my* schedule for the ten to twelve weeks of the season. Being a psychotherapist, I work two evenings a week. When the baseball season starts, I have to modify my evening schedule in order to be able to go to practice and then return to work for a couple of late-evening sessions. Perhaps if I were richer or more financially successful, I would not have to work those evenings. Unfortunately, as a result of the difference between the cost of living in the San Francisco Bay area and my wife's and my wages, I can't afford to lose the income from working those evenings. As in the stories I hear from so many fathers, we all learn to stretch ourselves to try and meet both the emotional and financial needs of our families.

Coaching baseball and softball is my most enjoyable "stretch." I am not a particularly avid fan of professional baseball, but the excitement of watching my children and their friends reminds me of all that is good and noble and engrossing about our national pastime. Both boys and girls bring to the game an energy and intensity that is very captivating and inspiring, and that their professional counterparts seem to lack. The lessons of life — working as a team, trying your best, learning how to lose, improving from your mistakes, enjoying personal success and sharing the pride of winning with friends — are all values that children's sports can bring us in contact with. The openness and naivete that each child brings to the game challenges me as a coach to respond with equal sensitivity to his or her honest emotions.

Observing the difference between girls' softball and boys' hardball allows me to see how gender differences are tied to the social conditioning that we are subject to.

Observing the difference between girls' softball and boys' hardball allows me to see how gender differences are tied to the social conditioning that we are subject to. Also, it is sad to see how boys are pushed to compete and win in order to prove their competence. I was not surprised to see that over 90% of the boys don't continue in organized sports after finishing Little League. I can remember when I played Little League thirty-five years ago. My coach interrogated me after I struck out because, he said, I did not show enough anger. I said I had tried my best, to which he responded that if I didn't get more upset after I struck out, he would take me out of the starting lineup. The next time I struck out I threw the bat against the bat rack, and the coach consoled me for my good try! I had obviously impressed him with my fake display of anger. It seemed as though this incident had convinced him that I had an intensity for the game.

As I began my Little League coaching career in AAA ball, the beginners' level, I went to view an upper-division game to see how it was coached. I was astonished to hear how the coach talked to the boys. Now, being a psychotherapist has it drawbacks, and perhaps having a natural interest in children's development makes me a bit more sensitive to how people communicate, but the criticism that was being leveled at the boys seemed extreme. When we began our season, I noticed distinct differences between coaching styles. Some of the men were without a doubt interested in supporting the boys at whatever level they could play, but others thought that winning was what it was all about. I was sure that I would be in the former group.

The only problem is that the final score never really tells you who won the game.

After our team lost its first four games, however, I found myself getting frustrated and wanting for my team to be "winners." It became easier to be disappointed in the boys when they missed a grounder, and harder and harder not to be discouraged after a poorly played inning. I found myself getting annoyed if the boys didn't play their hardest in each inning. I started to wonder what had happened to my own sensitivity and compassion. Where had I lost the conviction that it was just a game, and how had it become a contest? It was easy to get caught up in what I have always been trained to do, to be a "winner." The only problem is that the final score never really tells you who won the game. It took me years to learn this about life. I knew that I would like to be able to teach this to the children. Slowly, the art of coaching evolves, usually with the teamwork of the coaching staff. In Little League, it took working together and positive reinforcements from each coach on our team to preserve the fun in the game.

Coaching has challenged me to look at my own values about competition and winning.

I was surprised to see how critical the boys were of each other. A strike or a missed grounder was often met with laughter or a put-down. It took some time for the boys to learn to comfort each other. This was sad for me to see. When the boys were assured that they could comfort a friend who cried when he struck out, the feeling of being a team began to develop. Our society asks boys to be very independent and very competitive early in their lives. I think this makes it harder for them to be supportive of each other. To express their benevolent feelings for each other means showing tenderness and emotion. Boys are told that to be independent, they must give up this tender side of their characters. Being good means achieving "mastery" for boys — and this relates to being in control of their emotions. I think I was a good coach for the Little League because I took a positive stand and said that it was OK to cry and to be upset and to have your friends reassure you. Mind you, not all the coaches supported my position that winning wasn't what it was all about, but it certainly helped with my group's team spirit.

In my experience, girls' softball is a completely different story! Being involved with my daughter's softball teams during the last few years has been a real eye opener, showing me how positive sports can be. The league is organized around the idea that the game is fun. The coaches work cooperatively, and men and women coach together. The spirit of the girls as a team is present from the first day. The girls I have coached are in the second, third and fourth grades. I think two experiences I have had in coaching these girls sum up the differences between coaching the girls and coaching the boys.

First, I discovered that the girls do not want to get their friends "out" on the other teams. Last year, we had to spend the better part of one practice — an hour-and-a-half — talking about how it feels to "make an out" on a friend. I also found that if a girl gets hurt on the field, all the other girls run to her and try to help. We had to ask that just the two or three girls closest to her help out, to keep some order during the game. The sentiment of concern for teammates runs high. The social spirit of the game is intense and the competitiveness I have seen seems to be more in good fun and sport"than in winning and losing. The sense of mastery through winning does not appear to be a strong theme in girl's softball.

I know that I have oversimplified much of what goes on in Little League and girls softball. The point could be made that boys might gain from being less competitive and more team-oriented, and that girls could use a little more stimulation in the competitive realm. Of course, any of you who have coached know that coaching a team involves not only working with the children but working with the parents as well. The parents usually present the greater challenges. Coaching has challenged me to look at my own values about competition and winning. Sharing the experience with my kids has helped us all learn and struggle with what it means to be a team — which, come to think of it, is not so different from what it means to be a family!

FOR FURTHER SELF-REFLECTION AND DISCUSSION

1. How does competition effect boys' relationships with each other?

2. How do we create equal opportunity for our daughters to be physical,assertive and competitive?

3. What are your feelings about the importance of being part of a team? Do feel exercise and staying in shape ate important?

16

WHEN MEN BECOME FATHERS

THE OPPORTUNITIES FOR FATHERS TO PARTICIPATE in the early years of their children's lives appear to be becoming more important to men today. In the fathers' group I facilitate, many of the men comment on how they never had any close contact with their own fathers, and how that has made them painfully aware of how important it is to be present in their children's lives. Others say that, given the opportunity to choose between potential career advancement and spending time with their children, being with their kids feel like the more creative option.

Yet as most of us begin to explore what has been traditionally "women's territory," it is not an easy journey to undertake. Men I have worked with say that after trying to discover how to integrate a close relationship with their newborns, they often retreat to a more traditional role and begin to see themselves slowly becoming the distant fathers that they themselves knew.

It seems as if a natural bond occurs between women when they become mothers. A special way of knowing and sharing and deepening of friendships develops with other mothers.

We as men often seem to become more isolated from other men as family responsibilities and adjustments are made. We find that our work and family fill our time. We talk with our wives' friends, but why don't we seek out other fathers?

It has been my experience that when men become fathers, it is crucial to be around other fathers to share and explore this life transition.

Perhaps the way we as men are socialized to compete with other men has oppressed us to the point that we no longer are willing to take the risks of making new friendships. Maybe as we grope to discover our identities as fathers, we are too overwhelmed to reach out to other men. Maybe not having any role models for what kinds of friendships new fathers can have leads us to feel we must go it alone.

It has been my experience that when men become fathers, it is crucial to be around other fathers to share and explore this life transition. Fathers have something special to give each other.

Throughout history men have had opportunities to share with other men in a variety of different ways. It has only been during the last 60 years that the social climate has shifted in a way that isolates men from each other.

Through talking with other men about fatherhood we can begin to build a bridge back to the important relationships men can have with each other. We can begin to evolve a new model for how we can father.

Fathers meeting together and talking with other fathers is of great benefit, not only to us as men but to our children, our wives, our families, and ultimately to our culture and society as well.

FOR FURTHER SELF-REFLECTION AND DISCUSSION

1. How do you feel "connected" to, or companionship with, other men?

2. In an emergency, what male friend would you call first for help?

3. How do we as fathers develop supportive, caring, important relationships with other dads?

17

ANOTHER LOOK
AT FAMILY VALUES

LESS THAN 100 YEARS AGO, 90% of the U.S. population lived on farms. Most were subsistence farms, with the family needing to work together to fulfill the physical necessities of life. The family was also the center for education and learning. Family values were what you learned in the day-to-day working-out of life: understanding the changing seasons and the best time to plant crops or a garden, being able to recognize a good horse, and how to get along with your neighbor. These were the necessities for survival, but they also connected us to a deeper rhythm of life within the environment and our communities. The Bible was a popular tool for teaching reading and for community guidance (i.e., "Do unto others as you would want them to do unto you"), but the majority of Americans were not orthodox in their spiritual practices. The value of teamwork and collaboration in both the family and community was the central value for survival and living a civilized life. The rural home was the center of American life and culture; it was the productive center of our society. The farm provided everything needed to live. Survival and success were vitally linked to our relationships with others. It could be said that the value of cooperation within the family and the community, and with the land, was the principal "family value" in America at the turn of the century.

> **What I propose is that . . . we revitalize the family-farm value of cooperation.**

Today, less than 3% of our population lives on farms. Almost all farms today are part of agribusiness. There are few subsistence farms. The home today is not a place of production but the center of consumption. Beginning in the 1920s, industrial development jettisoned the father from the house and into the factory or office. Fifty years later, in the 1970s — just to "maintain" in our society of labor saving devices and conveniences — mothers joined dads in the work force. The values of a consumer society, based mainly on materialism, slowly became the dominant values for American families.

The satisfaction once experienced in relationships with family members, friends and communities has been replaced by the illusion of satisfaction through owning things. It has become so desirable to have a new car, the fastest computer, the latest CD, the most fashionable clothes, that people believe they will find satisfaction in life by possessing them. Commercial advertising, through the use of sophisticated psychological techniques, attempts to sell us products that will make us believe we are part of the "good life." The price the American family has paid for the good life has led us to be a nation suffering from depression.

We are lonely for each other and for a sense of being part of a greater community. Many people today long for a sense of community and personal attachment. We live in isolation from friends and family, and the need or desire for cooperation and teamwork as a family value has been replaced by the value of independence and self-sufficiency (especially emotionally). This profound change in the function of the home, from a center of productivity and connection to one of consumerism, has taken its toll on all of us as parents and partners (husbands and wives) but has affected our children most profoundly. Frustrated children, either in school or day care; long hours of watching television; parents exhausted by trying to make ends meet —- all of these have led us to our current discussion of family values in America.

Unfortunately, much of the family values movement offers an oversimplified response to helping our families. There is the mistaken notion that if the fathers are out there making a "good living" and mothers are in the home caring for children, we will regain a sense of balance in our society. Some of the leaders in this new movement try to use the Bible as the ultimate authority on how we need to organize our families. I wish the solution was so easy — that we could just look up what we need to do in a book!

The family has been and is a dynamic living organism. It has changed and adapted in the course of history to many different configurations. It exists today in many different paradigms throughout the world. In America we need to look at our own unique cultural and social conditions and ask ourselves what our families need now.

What I propose is that, on the personal level — on the simplest level — we revitalize the family-farm value of cooperation. Like the couples who ran family farms, we as parents can begin to work together as partners, looking at the demands and chores of life much as the farm families did. We need to ask how we can equitably share the tasks of sustaining a family. From earning our living to doing the laundry, we as parents can figure out how to navigate these tasks together. We can again learn how to reach out to our neighbors and friends, to help each other through the vicissitudes of modern life. We as families can learn to provide an environment in our daily lives that values cooperation and caring. We have to find the time, as families, to enjoy being together and sharing the events that shape our days. We want our children to be able to look to us, their parents, to have the skills and creativity to create a nurturing atmosphere.

The days of the father being at work and the mother staying home with the kids are gone, no longer a realistic model to emulate for parenting. As a family therapist, I often question whether it was ever the best model for raising children. But we have moved into new territory for parenting where, for both the satisfaction of the couple and survival of many families, men and women need to move toward learning how cooperation and teamwork can lead to enjoyment and satisfaction in life.

FOR FURTHER SELF-REFLECTION AND DISCUSSION

1. What is your response to the idea that family values are rooted in the cooperation between husband and wife?

2. What are three of the values that you and your partner convey to your children?

3. What will your child or children learn about family values by watching the relationship between you and your partner?

18

THE DIFFICULTIES OF LOVING

THERE IS NO MORE DIFFICULT TASK IN LIFE than having a satisfying marriage. As we approach Valentine's Day, our national holiday for celebrating the one we love, I think a closer look at how we can have a satisfying marriage might be valuable.

Divorce is a well-researched subject, but what it takes for a marriage to endure is less well understood. Many men and women feel that a personally satisfying marriage is not really possible, that marriage is something you tolerate in the service of raising children and being a family. Today there are both men and women who feel that the gender differences between the sexes make it impossible to expect that men and women can be emotionally close or intimate. As a family therapist, I have consulted with many couples who felt their own parents just survived being together but never experienced any real joy or energy in their marriage. Many individuals think they must give up on having a meaningful and fulfilling marriage and accept that raising children and finding some financial stability is the best they can hope for.

Not true! Although marriage is fragile and difficult, it is possible to understand how you can work toward a marriage that is inspiring and satisfying.

Life is difficult today. Economic demands are intense, and we face many competitive pressures. Our lives have become more and more impersonal. A marriage can become a refuge and oasis to help balance the depersonalizing forces assaulting our lives. If a man and woman choose to have children, they can make a connection with the continuity of time that raising children brings.

> *Divorce is a well-researched subject, but what it takes for a marriage to endure is less well understood.*

Not only is marriage a complex and fragile relationship, but perhaps more than at any other time in history it has become easy to give up on it and leave. Statistics do not look good: 50% of marriages end in divorce. In the past, law, religion, traditions and family values helped to keep people trying to work on their relationships. Today, staying married is totally voluntary. The ease of getting a divorce allows couples to quickly and simply decide they want out.

There is no other relationship, no other endeavor we undertake in life, about which we get less information than marriage. Little instruction, less information and few role models exist to help guide us through the often stormy waters. Marriage, I believe, is a doorway to a truly deeper understanding of ourselves as we struggle to make our relationship with our partner work. Being able to acknowledge our conflicts, and to struggle with those conflicts in the relationship, takes courage and hope. The subtle childhood needs we bring to our marriages cause tension and also point to the creative edge of our own personal growth.

We are not prepared for this kind of "work." We are taught to view marriage as something that will bestow happiness and fulfillment upon us. We are not told that learning to love another person will be difficult, tiring and frustrating. We tend to miss the cues that let us know that the problems in a marriage are really attempts to move closer, to be understood better, to be more intimate with our partners.

Marriage is an ongoing, lifelong process of working on something that is greater than either one of the individuals involved. It is more than a commitment to another person. It is a journey with specific landmarks and developmental transitions. Judith Wallerstein and Sandra Blakeslee, in their new book *The Good Marriage*, have outlined nine tasks with which every marriage must struggle.

> **Marriage is an ongoing, lifelong process of working on something that is greater than either one of the individuals involved.**

The first stage, according to Wallerstein and Blakeslee, is working out the separation from each person's family of origin. There is so much we just assume about life and relationships. Having some psychological understanding of these forces can free us to connect with our partners in a more open and authentic way. The next stage is the struggle with our needs for autonomy and togetherness, and with it the need to balance our domestic life and our need for individual growth as part of the relationship. The third task is struggling with the decision of whether or not to be parents. Either road taken can lead to a fulfilling and satisfying life. The task is how the couple works out this important life decision. All relationships also have crises, deaths, illnesses and job losses, and how a couple works through these events is the fourth task. The fifth task, say Wallerstein and Blakeslee, is making a safe place for conflict. Having trust that you can argue with your partner, and that both you and the relationship will survive, is important in creating this place. Exploring the sexuality of marriage is the sixth task. As a family therapist, I often see couples who come into therapy struggling with this. Sexuality seems to open discussions on many of the other tasks the relationship is working on. Sharing laughter and keeping individual and common interests alive is the seventh task. Finding life stimulating and having a sense of humor is a vital ingredient for longevity in a marriage. The eighth task is providing emotional nurturing. This comes with really feeling that your partner "sees" you. Do you and your partner feel an empathetic connection — being understood for how you feel, free of judgements and criticism? The ninth and final task is how to provide for a "double vision." This double vision shows us where we started in a relationship and where our lives are now. It also shows us how much can evolve in the living of a lifetime with someone. These tasks don't occur in a linear fashion, but overlap and recur, to be worked on again over the course of time.

Wallerstein and Blakeslee have created a terrific map to view marriage, and traveling through the countryside of marriage can be a great adventure. Although the tasks of marriage are difficult, having committed yourself to loving another person is truly the most noble of all our human endeavors.

FOR FURTHER SELF-REFLECTION AND DISCUSSION

1. What "stages" that Wallerstein and Blakeslee describe are you "working through?"

2. Why is loving another person so difficult?

3. How do you feel about the way your parents expressed their caring for and "loving" each other in their marriage?

(Note: *The Good Marriage: How and Why Love Lasts*, by Judith Wallerstein and Sandra Blakeslee, was published by Houghton Mifflin, New York, in 1995.)

19

SEX AND PARENTHOOD

HAVING A BABY AND MAKING THE TRANSITION TO PARENTHOOD is a very complicated process. I say this from both my professional perspective as a family counselor and my own experience as a father of a 10- and 14-year-old. With all the various pressures on young families, there is often not enough time or energy for parents to have the sexual contact one or both partners desire. As I look back on my marriage (and it's still true today), both my wife and I have had to discuss and accommodate our personal needs and desires, as well as the logistics of work schedules and kids' schedules, to find the time and "timing" to be together sexually.

Before we had kids, which seems like another lifetime now, our sexual relationship was fairly spontaneous. We had time together most evenings, and we were young and had less complicated professional and emotional commitments. Over the years together, just being parents has changed our emotional dispositions, our bodies and our desires for sex. After eighteen years together, we are truly different people than we were when we first met. Our sexual relationship has in its frequency and intensity been rather unpredictable. I have tried to keep an open dialogue about how I feel about our sexual relationship, but at times it has been difficult to discuss. I think each of us has been concerned about hurting the other in discussing our sexual need. My wife and I continue today to struggle with our sexual desires and our needs for intimacy while we try to understand our individual differences, what we need in terms of sex, and how to feel close and connected in our marriage.

> *I have tried to keep an open dialogue about how I feel about our sexual relationship.*

How important is sex to a marriage? Sex seems to be the emotional barometer for most marriages. Not in the sense that the more sex the better the marriage, but in the way couples can discuss openly and with concern for each other their feelings about the intimacy in their relationship. In this way, sexuality is a symbolic way each partner becomes emotionally vulnerable. As a psychotherapist, I am acutely aware that each individual's ability to be emotionally vulnerable is often more a reflection of the influences of the family he or she grew up in than of feelings about a current relationship or spouse.

I find in my work that in the couple's relationship, the individuals are working out the intimacy (or lack of it) that they experienced in their own family of origin. Although couples will focus the tension in their relationship on sexuality, that is often a reflection of feelings of being appreciated and understood. What psychotherapists call "being seen" by one's partner — a sense that the other person understands or empathizes with your experience, separate from his or her own — appears to be a significant building block for emotional intimacy. As my clients report to me, there is a high correlation between this type of being seen and sexual intimacy and desire.

In working with fathers I have noticed a few particular themes in regard to sexuality. Some men have difficulty adjusting to the change in their wive's body shape after the birth of a baby. With all the advertising and media hype about how women's bodies should look, the whole Playboy image can create problems for men (and women). Fathers often need to free themselves from the fantasies of the commercialism of women's sexuality to appreciate the reality of their wife's sexuality. During pregnancy, some men begin to resent the attention their wives get. They can develop an underlying anger that can become a powerful inhibitor to feelings of sexuality. After the baby is born the two-person bond is shifted. A new father often feels excluded by his wife's attention to their newborn. This can lead to feelings of anger, sadness, and depression. Oftentimes these feelings are expressed by either emotional or physical withdrawal. Many men (and women, too) aren't consciously aware of these feelings. It can be difficult to talk about these feelings, even if the parents are aware of

> *At various times in a relationship, couples feel the need to put their sexuality on hold while they are working through other issues in their relationship or life.*

them. Especially in the early years, when most fathers are trying to find their place in their families, they may feel it would be a burden on the relationship to discuss the way they feel. They may even feel guilty for having the feelings.

Some men feel uncomfortable about having sex during pregnancy. They have fears they will be hurting the baby or their partners. Many men need to look at how they view their own bodies in relationship to a pregnancy. If, during the pregnancy (this can also be true throughout the marriage), a man's partner agrees to accommodate his physical needs but isn't interested herself in lovemaking, how should he feel? If he is enjoying himself and she isn't, should he feel guilty? Is this kind of sexuality OK?

Is sex necessary? For some couples, it is critical to have an active sex life. It serves as both a physical and emotional outlet for tension. For other couples, the fun and excitement they experience through sex is very important. While many couples need to have sexual intercourse to feel satisfied, other couples find cuddling and holding will suffice. At various times in a relationship, couples feel the need to put their sexuality on hold while they are working through other issues in their relationship or life.

There are many legitimate forms of love-making that we overlook. Stress and tension in life are often relieved by feelings of closeness and by holding and touching another human being (most often our partners). Kissing, massage and mutual masturbation are all ways to fulfill physical desires we all normally need to express.

Through working with the sexuality in our marriages we learn about so many things: our needs for closeness and intimacy, our own desires and our own bodies. By discussing these feelings with our partners we gain perspective and develop emotional maturity. We learn that our sexual desires and needs can be a doorway to a deeper understanding of our partners and ourselves.

FOR FURTHER SELF-REFLECTION AND DISCUSSION

1. How has the sexuality in your relationship changed since you had a child?

2. Do you know other dads or men with whom you can talk about your sexual feelings in your marriage?

3. How important to you is the sexual relationship in your marriage?

20

What My Son Taught Me About Being a Man: Vague Ramblings of the Father of a Nine-Year-Old Boy

Our son Morgan is nine now. Since his birth I have actively participated in his care. This has not always been easy. I think my first lesson was that men as fathers are expected to help their wives but not be too interested in actually caring for their children. Fathers should be helpful around the house but not wander too far into "women's territory."

When Morgan was a baby, I worked only part-time so I could share equally in his care. We made daily journeys to the park. We played in the sand with his trucks and talked with the moms who were there. Because I was the only man at the park with my kid, the consensus or assumption was that I was taking care of my child because I was unemployed.

I remember talking with a grandmother who was at the park. I told her that my wife and I both worked part-time, that we didn't need to hire childcare and that I felt fortunate to be able to spend this time with my son, especially while he was a baby. She listened attentively. As I left the park she told me how much she had enjoyed talking with me, and said she hoped I would be able to get more work soon!

I lost count of the number of times women said how nice it was to see a man "mothering." I usually responded that they were actually observing fathering. I was not attempting to be a role model or make a political statement about men as fathers. I was taking action on what was important and meaningful to me.

I lost count of the number of times women said how nice it was to see a man "mothering."

So this was my first lesson. Procreation was part of being a man. Feeling one's potency through conception, this was definitely masculine. Yet wanting to care for a baby — no, this was not what being a man was about. At least that was the message I was getting. But that was just the beginning.

These early years with my son were wonderful and exciting — and like living with a Zen master. Morgan, like all young children, lived totally in the present. With him I learned about plants, bugs, flowers, cracks in the cement, and all the little details of life and our environment that usually passed me by.

It was when Morgan entered school that I got my real insight into what it means to grow up male in America. Boys and girls are different. Just go to any elementary school and it is easy to verify this. It also became evident that active and energetic boys are sometimes troubling for teachers. They can't sit still. Their curiosity is insatiable, and most teachers (who are usually women) may not be tolerant of their exuberance.

Morgan had studied Martin Luther King and the Civil Rights Movement in the second grade. On our way home from school one day, Morgan told me that in his class the boys where being treated like the blacks in the South whom Martin Luther King was trying to help. I asked him what he meant. He said that if the girls talked out of turn or didn't listen, the teacher would ask them to please be quiet. If the boys did the same thing, she would yell at them and be very angry about how bad they were.

Shaming starts early. To be a man in America means to grow up with a large dose of shame — shame about your energy and desire and shame about your body. Morgan's experiences began to remind me of what I had heard so often in school as a child: "You're too excited and you can't sit still. What's wrong with you that you can't sit still?" What was wrong with me because I got too excited? Why was it bad to feel this way? What a terrible body I must have, that I couldn't sit without mov-

> *The shaming, the competitiveness we experience as children, cuts us off from appreciating ourselves and others.*

ing. If the words themselves weren't shaming, the tone was.

Morgan has learned many wonderful things in school, and he has developed and worked out many important relationships. He has had great, mediocre and bad teachers. My wife and I have tried to guide him to situations that were socially and academically life-enhancing. I would be in denial not to say that boys are treated very differently in school than girls are. At least at the elementary level. And so much of our creativity and feeling is shamed out of us. The exuberance of a third- or fourth-grade boy is a dangerous experience.

The next insight on what it means to be a man has to do with competition. I am amazed and appalled by the level of competitiveness I see among young boys. It begins with athletics and then permeates all other aspects of their lives. What I see is that by the fourth grade a pecking order — a hierarchy — is already established. That hierarchy seems to grant each child a limited potential of feelings and expression. It is the beginning of our life-long experience with isolation from our peers. In my son's case, I see the absence of adult males in any other area than athletics. There are so few men in the schools to model other ways of being and feeling.

The competitiveness goes far beyond athletics. Who has the best new toy? Whether it concerns a new book or a new Nintendo game, there is a real lack of appreciation for the other boy's experience. It becomes threatening to these eight- and nine-year-olds if a friend has something of value.

How well that translates to my experience as an adult male and the difficulty I see in myself, sometimes, in being able to support and appreciate the achievements of other men. I understand this intellectually, but on a feeling level it runs deep. Watching my son's experience with his friends, it is obvious how I learned these feelings.

At Morgan's ninth birthday party, he had ten of his friends sleep over. In the morning, the "gang," as we called ourselves, walked to the bakery. On the way home, one of the boys tripped on the sidewalk and fell. He was crying. Immediately everyone laughed and made fun of him. They had learned it is shameful to cry and were shaming their friend with laughter. I held the hurt boy. I called all the other boys around me. I told them that the men I know would help out a friend if he was hurt. I said "real" men would show their strength by caring about what happened to a friend.

I was not prepared for their response. They began to ask their crying friend where his hurt was. They crowded around and put their arms around him. As we continued to walk home, each boy talked with him individually about his tripping on the sidewalk. The whole interaction shifted, and I don't think it was due to the "eloquence" of what I had said.

It became apparent that these boys had absorbed what I said as if it were water and they were walking through a desert. They thirsted for some validation from an adult male who would say that it is alright to have concerned feelings for a hurt friend. It's OK to cry. I am sure they all knew the loneliness of being teased when they got hurt. I just told them that men care about their friends and show concern about what happens to them. A simple message.

Where are the men — fathers, brothers, uncles, cousins, neighbors, mentors, political leaders and teachers — to carry this simple message to our children?

The shaming, the competitiveness we experience as children, cuts us off from appreciating ourselves and others. My son has, through his journey, reminded me of how painful a process it is for boys to grow up in America. I hope that by participating in his life I have helped him to develop some skillful means for finding antidotes to shaming and competitiveness. By being present in his life, and with the help of my male friends, I hope he will see a wide range and depth of feeling experienced and expressed by different men.

Perhaps growing up male in America is basically an abusive experience. We as men can help each other recover from our shame and competitive/isolating lives. (Much has been said about this in the recent men's movement.) Let us begin our own healing by respecting and nurturing the sons, daughters and children that we know.

FOR FURTHER SELF-REFLECTION AND DISCUSSION

1. What feelings do you have about this essay?

2. Do you remember any similar situations from your childhood?

3. Can men be strong, tender and masculine at the same?

Appendix
The Fathers' Forum

I started the Fathers' Forum in 1986 with the belief that our lives as fathers could be more meaningful, vital, interesting and enjoyable if we had preparation for becoming parents. This included being prepared for and actively involved in the birth process. It meant learning about the transition to parenthood and how the difficult first year of parenthood affects us as men. And finally it includes re-examining our relationships with other men and appreciating the value of male friendships, especially learning how to develop friendships with other fathers and being able to discuss with them our personal feelings about parenting and fatherhood.

I designed the Fathers' Forum to address these aspects of men's development through classes, workshops and groups for fathers. Although still a "work in progress," the Fathers' Forum — through support from birth/parent educators and local hospitals as well as interest from community organizations — has continued to evolve in Northern California, in the United States.

Currently the Fathers' Forum offers the following programs:

"Becoming a Father"
Making the transition to parenthood

We live in a society and culture that does little to prepare us as men for the important experience of childbirth and the transition to parenthood. This two-and-a-half-hour class is designed to help men understand how the process of childbirth and becoming a father may affect them. Come join us as we discuss the emotional and social adjustments men experience in the process of becoming a father. At the conclusion of this class the expectant father should 1) be more confident about the childbirth process and 2) feel reduced stress and anxiety about becoming a father.

"Discovering Fatherhood"
An all-day workshop for expectant and new fathers

In this six-hour workshop we meet together, as a community of fathers, to consider what "being a father" means to each of us personally. Through videos, presentations and discussion we explore the profound transition a man goes through when he becomes a father.

Men's Groups for Fathers
Ongoing bimonthly group for fathers with young children

In the Fathers' Forum Men's Groups we discuss our hopes, aspirations, dreams and disappointments about fatherhood. These groups explore the cultural and social myths about fatherhood, our relationships with our own fathers, how having a baby changes the relationship with our partners, balancing career and family life, sexuality after children, expressing anger and frustration, and the diversity of parenting styles for fathers. The groups are limited to seven men.

You can reach the Fathers' Forum at (510) 644-0300 or on the Internet at www.fathersforum.com.

About the Author

Bruce Linton, Ph.D., founded the Fathers' Forum, which offers workshops, classes and groups for expectant and new fathers. Bruce is a licensed marriage, family and child counselor and received his doctorate for research on men's development as fathers. He was a contributing editor to *Full-Time Dads* magazine and a former a columnist for *Children's News* in San Francisco. Bruce has a private counseling and psychotherapy practice in Berkeley, California, where he lives with his wife and two children. Bruce is a popular speaker at conferences, hospitals, corporations and community organizations.

Order Form

Copies of *Finding Time for Fatherhood: The Important Considerations Men Face When They Become Fathers,* by Bruce Linton, Ph.D., are available for $12.95 each (price includes sales tax) plus shipping and handling.

 TELEPHONE or **ON-LINE ORDERS**. Have your VISA, MasterCard, AMEX, Optima or Discover card ready.

TELEPHONE: Call *toll-free*, 1-888-706-1199

INTERNET: www.fathersforum.com

✉ **MAIL** or **FAX ORDERS**. Send a copy of this form.

FAX: (510) 845-8530

MAIL: Fathers' Forum Press
1521-A Shattuck Ave., Suite 201
Berkeley, CA 94709-1516

Your Name _____

Address_____

City _____ State _____ Zip _____

Telephone (_____) _____

Please send me _____ copies X $12.95 = $ _____
(Price includes applicable sales tax)

Shipping and handling for the *first* book: $ 1.50

Shipping and handling for
each *additional* book: _____ copies X $ .75 = $ _____

Total | $ _____ |

Payment method (credit card *only* for fax orders):

CHECK ❏ (please enclose with order)

CREDIT CARD: ❏ VISA ❏ MasterCard ❏ AMEX ❏ Optima ❏ Discover

Card number _____

Name on card _____ Exp. date _____ / _____

Order Form

Copies of *Finding Time for Fatherhood: The Important Considerations Men Face When They Become Fathers,* by Bruce Linton, Ph.D., are available for $12.95 each (price includes sales tax) plus shipping and handling.

 TELEPHONE or **ON-LINE ORDERS**. Have your VISA, MasterCard, AMEX, Optima or Discover card ready.

TELEPHONE: Call *toll-free*, 1-888-706-1199

INTERNET: www.fathersforum.com

MAIL or **FAX ORDERS**. Send a copy of this form.

FAX: (510) 845-8530

MAIL: Fathers' Forum Press
1521-A Shattuck Ave., Suite 201
Berkeley, CA 94709-1516

Your Name _____

Address _____

City _____ State _____ Zip _____

Telephone (_____) _____

Please send me _____ copies X $12.95 = $ _____
(Price includes applicable sales tax)

Shipping and handling for the *first* book: $ 1.50

Shipping and handling for
each *additional* book: _____ copies X $ .75 = $ _____

Total | $ |

Payment method (credit card *only* for fax orders):

CHECK ❏ (please enclose with order)

CREDIT CARD: ❏ VISA ❏ MasterCard ❏ AMEX ❏ Optima ❏ Discover

Card number _____

Name on card _____ Exp. date _____ / _____